A history of
WOODCHESTER MANSION
and a photographic record from 1987 to 2013

"Inscribe all human effort with one word,
Artistry's haunting curse – the Incomplete!"

Robert Browning (1871)

PHOTOGRAPHY by MARGARET LISTER
EDITED by JOHN FULLARD

Published by Benwell Publishing
ISBN 978-0-9929156-0-5
© Margaret Lister 2014

All photographs are by Margaret Lister
unless stated otherwise.

Acknowledgements
    English Heritage
    Liz Davenport
    Mike Hill

CONTENTS

MARGARET LISTER

One of the founder members of the Woodchester Mansion Trust and a resident of Woodchester for over forty years. A professional photographer, having graduated with a BA Hons in Fine Art. Tutor in Photography at Stroud College for twenty years and ran workshops at the Royal Photographic Society. Work exhibited widely around the south west region, with special interest in landscape and architectural photography. Photographs for *Cotswold Stone Homes* by Mike Hill, Sally Birch and Margaret Lister, published 1994.

JOHN FULLARD

Architectural graduate – winner of Aaron Memorial Scholarship for dissertation on history of English seaside piers. Worked in local authority and private architectural practices – projects include the Harrogate Conference Centre and the Arundel WWT Visitor Centre. Moved into construction publishing, first with the Royal Institute of British Architects, then working with agencies in London and Cheltenham.

BIBLIOGRAPHY

Woodchester History
   Rev WNRJ Black
Victorian Architecture
   Roger Dixon & Stefan Muthesius
The Age of Revolution: Europe 1789–1848
   Eric Hobsbawm

Country Houses of Gloucestershire Vol 3
   Nicholas Kingsley & Michael Hill
Gloucestershire. 1, The Costwolds (Pevsner's *Buildings of England* series)
   David Verey & Alan Brooks
Publications produced by The Woodchester Mansion Trust
   (www.woodchestermansion.org.uk)

WOODCHESTER MANSION – AN UNFINISHED GOTHIC MASTERPIECE

"Inscribe all human effort with one word, Artistry's haunting curse - the Incomplete!"
Robert Browning (1871)

In 1987 a small group of historic building enthusiasts visited Woodchester Mansion. One of this visiting group was professional photographer Margaret Lister, and this visit marked the beginning of her long-running photographic and personal interest in the Mansion and the spiritual community that grew up around it.

This elegant, enigmatically 'incomplete' Victorian Gothic country house had been unoccupied for the best part of a century, hidden away in a secluded south Cotswolds valley, totally neglected and largely forgotten, except by a small group of dedicated bat conservationists whose interests lay in the natural, rather than the built, environment. As a result of their shared interest in the building the members got together to form the Woodchester Mansion Conservation Group in 1988, which became the Woodchester Mansion Trust in 1992. The trust pays the Mansion's owners, Stroud District Council, a peppercorn rent of just £1 a year for a 99-year lease.

As the Council was looking to hand over the maintenance of the building, the Woodchester Mansion Conservation Group presented a feasibility study with the aim of repairing the building to its unfinished state, training students in

▲ Woodchester Mansion — with its ground floor windows boarded up — as photographed in 1987 from the south ridge, looking north, a view now hidden by the intervening years of tree growth.

▲ A 1904 picture postcard of 'The Mansion, Woodchester Park' bearing the sender's question, "Do you know this place [?]" — which carries with it some hint of mystery?

stonemasonry skills, and opening the building to the public.

In 1994, the National Trust bought Woodchester Park, so that the grounds were also accessible to the public.

The driving force behind Woodchester Park's Victorian Gothic mansion was William Leigh, made wealthy thanks to a substantial inheritance from his father—a successful Liverpool merchant—who died in 1815, when his son was only thirteen. Thirty years later William Leigh converted to the Roman Catholic Church. After his conversion, Leigh developed a powerful personal vision of establishing a new Catholic community in an area where none existed, his chosen location being Woodchester in Gloucestershire. The focus of this project would be his own country house, the scale and style of which would be a worthy reflection of his zeal for his new-found faith.

Living in Staffordshire, Leigh had met another Catholic convert, architect Augustus Wellesley Northmore Pugin, for whom Gothic architecture was the only style he considered to be a true reflection of their shared religion. We will hear more later of their association, for Pugin would produce the very first Gothic-style design for William Leigh's proposed mansion.

Client and architect later parted company and that design was never realised. Other architects followed, but, for a devout William Leigh, the Gothic style remained the building's essential characteristic, the one and only architectural style that he saw as a true expression of his Catholic faith.

Leigh bought the estate in 1845 and construction work on the new mansion began in the mid-1850s, following the design of yet another Catholic convert, 21 year-old local architect Benjamin Bucknall. By 1873, when William Leigh died, construction work had stopped and it seems that successive generations of the Leigh family lacked the funds and the motivation to take the project through to completion. The Leigh family eventually faded away—with male heirs suffering illness and premature death—the line ending with the post-war death of two spinster sisters, who had, by then, sold the Mansion. Woodchester Mansion remains to this day as Bucknall's unfinished Victorian Gothic masterpiece that has been deliberately maintained since the late 1980s to conserve its unfinished state.

The Mansion's 'rediscovery' in 1987 was timely, in that the seemingly inevitable descent to dereliction was finally checked after years of neglect. Its overall condition might have been far worse, but in the 1950s, Reginald Kelly had taken the lease of the Mansion and tried to keep the roof in good condition. In the mid-1970s Mr Kelly, took on essential basic maintenance, such as clearing gutters — so at least the mansion's main fabric remained more or less intact during the years of abandonment. The house was also protected from the very worst vandalism and the risk of unsympathetic development by the post-war private ownership of the land and the remote situation of the Mansion, deep in the valley and about a mile from the nearest road in the village of Nympsfield and some three miles from Woodchester village.

So, in 1987, when the group made their early, exploratory visits, they found an elegant but abandoned building site — ground floor windows were boarded up and haphazard barricades blocked other points of entry; old wooden ladders and timber arch formworks were still in place and working tools had been left lying around. Immediately inside the entrance, a towering three-storey open space awaited the insertion of its floors, with gaping fireplaces marking each proposed level above.

▲ Despite rudimentary maintenance by the Mansion's tenant in the 1950s and '60s, by the time this 1987 photograph was taken of the North Range — the servants' quarters and domestic areas — the process of dereliction was well advanced.

4

The Dining Room awaits its vaulted ceiling: the supporting floor structure to the bedroom above, with the old ladder and the timber centering formwork for the main arch both still propped in place. ▷

Margaret Lister's photographs dating from this period of 'rediscovery' — many previously unpublished — record the state of the mansion as she found it in the late 1980s. Through her explorations of the Mansion, she developed an interest in the Leigh family's influence on the wider Woodchester community which subsequently afforded her a unique opportunity to record life in the closed order of the Sisters of Poor Clares at the convent *[see page 30]*. First, let us revisit Woodchester Mansion and see the building as she saw it through her camera lens all those years ago.

5

▲ Up into the void — this towering three-storey space greets the visitor immediately on entering through the west door, with gaping fireplaces announcing the missing floors above. At ground floor level, this was planned as the Hall and Billiard Room. The unplastered walls reveal the normally hidden details of construction, such as the rough brick relieving arches each transferring masonry loads sideways and downwards around the elegantly carved stone fireplaces.

▲ The raised door threshold leads from the Library into the wood-floored Drawing Room beyond. The lower earth floor, with glimpses of the shallow vault structure below, reveal the prevailing unfinished state of the ground floor. Even over a relatively small opening, the builders used the structural device of a relieving arch. First floor level would have been immediately above the carved stone window arch.

Windows boarded up, its fine details in shadow—in 1987, this was the Drawing Room, the one major space, complete with a floor. It was dressed in preparation for a visiting cardinal, albeit in 1894, twenty years after William Leigh's death, twenty years after building work stopped.

WHY BUILD THE MANSION THERE?

The position of an existing 17th century house on the site is possibly the one very practical reason for the siting of Woodchester Mansion, but the choice remains something of an enigma.

Woodchester Mansion was built on the same site as the demolished Georgian house built by the previous owners, the Ducie family. It is thought that the Ducie family's Georgian mansion had 'grown' from an old hunting Lodge that was already on the site when the family bought the estate in the 17th century. The Victorian building stands within the valley that runs west to east, from the village of Nympsfield, down to Woodchester. But the choice of this site within the huge area of available parkland begs the question: why was this site chosen?

The mansion sits at a narrow point between the steep sides of the valley and often the house stands in shade, sunless in the depths of winter, in the shadow of the rising profile of the ridge to the south. The orientation of the building on the site compounds these limitations: the south elevation looks across a narrow part of the valley to the shaded ridge to the south. The site is something of a gloomy basin, where frost and mist can linger, offering little comfort—an important consideration, given that Leigh suffered from chest problems.

In his very first quotation for the building of William Leigh's mansion—dated 15th January 1846—architect AWN Pugin sowed the seeds of retaining the Ducie Mansion site, based on the material practicalities that it presented. In the estimate he schedules the cost benefits of re-using or selling salvaged stone and other materials from the existing mansion and associated service buildings, for example:

"There is in fact oak enough to lay all the best bedrooms and dressing rooms of the new house as well as the lower rooms."

Pugin's estimate unequivocally opts for demolition from the start—at an estimated cost of £420—and then building anew on the Ducie site. One major factor in 'fixing' this as the new building's location, was his suggestion that the Ducie cellars should be retained and reused, saving the cost of excavating tonnes of earth. Cellars were essential to Victorian households, offering the only form of cool summer storage within domestic buildings; a separate ice house was built outside, a major construction dug deep into the ground.

So, while there might have been issues concerning the site's micro-climate, the Ducie mansion site offered one eminently practical option for the Leigh family and their architect. Here was a prepared, levelled site, with ready-made cellars, affording builders tonnes of salvaged stone and other materials.

▲ In what would have been the Mansion's principal service room — the Kitchen — casements swing open, windows have been smashed and the room has been used as a lumber dump.

▲ As an indication of the basic essentials required of Mansion repairs, here is the same window in the cleared Kitchen — photographed some years later — with new glazing to keep out the prevailing cold and damp of the valley beyond.

This was the condition of the Chapel in 1987, with the west rose window clearly visible through the smashed glazing of the east window. Since 1992, the Chapel has been shrouded in scaffolding and an over-roof awning, awaiting repair ▶

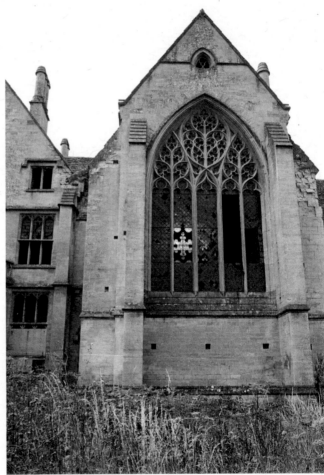

▼ The west Rose Window photographed in 1987, showing the poor state of the fabric, with dampness staining the ceiling vaults, cracked and missing stones, broken windows and a general air of dereliction — echoed in the photograph of the east window *[below right]*.

FAITH

"Gothic architecture is the only correct expression of the faith, wants, and climate of our country ... whilst we glory in being Englishmen, let us have an architecture, the arrangement and details of which alike remind us of our [Catholic] faith and our country."

Apology for the Revival of Christian Architecture in England by AWN Pugin (1843)

In 1845, while living in Staffordshire, William Leigh converted to the Roman Catholic church, an act of faith that shaped the rest of his life, leading to his move to Gloucestershire and the construction of Woodchester Mansion, even dictating its Gothic style.

Leigh asked the architect AWN Pugin, another devout Catholic convert, to prepare designs for Woodchester in 1846. As an architect, Pugin aligned his Catholic faith completely with Gothic architecture, to the extent that he saw Georgian neo-classical buildings—such as the estate's existing Ducie mansion—as totally inappropriate, even immoral because of their associations with *'pagan worship'* (*True Principles of Pointed Architecture*). As the reign of George IV was coming to an end, Pugin was among a new generation of bright young *'men of large designs'* who totally rejected the neo-classical style.

For Pugin, the Gothic arch pointed the way towards heaven and he saw it as the most spiritual form of architecture. In his view, it represented the traditions associated with 'Catholic Christianity', which had prevailed in England prior to the Reformation. He came to regard the Gothic style as the very pinnacle of human achievement, an expression of faith through artistic creativity. In intellectual circles of the time, the theme of contrast between the 'goodness' of the

Middle Ages and the 'degeneracy' of the Georgian era was widely accepted. Pugin sought to express this 'goodness' by designing in true Gothic style.

William Leigh—*"a man of solid piety and unbounded generosity to the church and the poor"*—established Nympsfield and South Woodchester as centres for Catholic worship. He was awarded the Order of St. Gregory by Pope Pius IX in recognition of this work.

There is a school of thought that always believed that Leigh intended his mansion as a refuge for the Pope himself, at a time of great instability in Italy, with the Pope under direct threat from Republican upheavals. Letters exist in the Vatican archives from the nephew of the Prime Minister, Lord Russell, stating that Pius IX had enquired about the possibility of seeking sanctuary in England.

During 1848 the level of public disorder grew in Italy; on November 15, the Prime Minister was murdered during riots; the Pope was trapped in his palace by the mob and forced to flee Rome in disguise on November 24. He did not return to Rome until April 1850, and then only after he had called upon Napoleon III's troops to crush the Republicans.

While events in Italy ran parallel to Leigh's early visions for the mansion under the auspices of Pugin, the Pope had been reinstated by the time Leigh met Benjamin Bucknall (1852) and it was

1857 before he began work on the design. So the papal refuge theory as Leigh's motivation for building the Mansion seems flawed by virtue of simple chronology.

▲ The tomb of William Leigh—"a man of solid piety"—in the church he built in south Woodchester; holding a replica of his own Woodchester Mansion.

The Chapel, south window: further evidence of decay and neglect, showing how vulnerable the unfinished building was, exposed to the worst effects of the elements for more than one hundred years.

Elsewhere within the Chapel, unaffected by the elements, these delicately carved details are as crisp and fresh as the day the Victorian stonemason completed them in the 19th century.

▼ Despite the prevailing air of dereliction, what stands out is the cleverly detailed, carefully crafted interlocking arch structures forming the staircase up to the Ironing Room...

▼ Looking along the ground floor's west/east corridor from the Hall and Billiard Room towards the boarded-up windows of the east elevation. The 'floor' in this 1987 photograph is formed by the shallow arches of the cellar vaults below – since masked by new flooring. The second pool of light on the left is the entrance to the Grand Stair.

13

THE GRAND STAIR

The Grand Stair had been virtually completed by 1873, but since then has been badly affected by many years of damaging exposure to wind, rain and frost.

▼ The top landing of the Grand Stair, open to the elements with all its windows broken.

▲ The Grand Stair window, looking out into the central quadrangle — the head of the window, including the central keystone, has collapsed, crudely propped by a length of timber. Incoming rain and winter frosts have combined to blow cracks in the columns and erode and flake the internal faces of the dressed stone.

▲ Looking down the Grand Stair from the landing *[left]* the unplastered walls show the use of a relieving arch above the opening for the internal windows.

Before — as it was in 1987 — and some years later ▼, the Grand Stair, showing the difficult balance between effective repair and renovation and maintaining the building's status quo as an unfinished Gothic-style construction.

 Echoing the interlocking arch structures of the Laundry Room (Page 13) this is the servants' stair connecting to the first floor.

A crude barricade jammed in place in the window of the first floor Bathroom in an attempt to keep out would-be vandals. ▶

▼ The first-floor bedroom as found in 1987, lacking its ceiling, with the timber centering frame removed from the completed central arch by the builders and left on the floor.

▼ The same room, seen from above and several years later, after rubbish and debris has been cleared to reveal the vaulted construction of the room below. Compare the fine detail of the arch's carved stone with the bulk of the roughly fashioned centering formwork.

▲ The vaulting detail, showing the brick infill between the ribs and the central boss feature which 'locks' the whole structure together.

17

▲ The Ironing Room shown here just as it was found in 1987, with clear indications among the detritus that it had been used by Vincent Leigh as an improvised laboratory, while he lived in the Mansion in the 1900s.

▼ The Ironing Room, some years later, cleaned up and used by stonemasonry students as a meeting room.

▲ Another detail in the Ironing Room: the floating circular 'window' formed by the graceful double-arched structure, growing out of the simply carved central column.

THE SECOND FLOOR

▼ The second-floor Brewery reveals the soaring structural spans that are one of the key architectural features of the Mansion's construction; this area is open to visitors only on rare occasions.

BATS IN THE ATTIC…
Horseshoe bats at Woodchester Mansion

Greater and Lesser Horseshoe bats (both endangered, two of the UK's 17 bat species) are believed to have roosted at Woodchester Mansion since the 1950s. They arrive in April or May and use the mansion as a 'Delivery Room', a safe place to have their pups in June and July, most leaving in September to hibernate.

Since 1959, Greater Horseshoe bats have been studied at Woodchester Mansion by Dr Roger Ramsome and a team of volunteers. Each species roosts in its designated 'Bat Attic', both covered by night-vision cameras so conservationists and the public can view the process of 'bringing up bat baby'. Colonies have grown significantly since the 1960s — almost 300 adult and baby Greater Horseshoe bats were recorded in 2011.

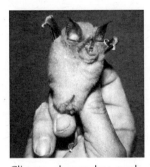

Climate change has probably assisted this positive development, with some agricultural assistance, as the meadows around the Mansion are grazed by arrangement with a local farmer so that the resulting cow dung will attract feeding dung beetles, a major food source for the bats. In 2013, a programme of plantation tree clearance was begun, which should also help to increase Horseshoe bat numbers, as dense woodland is not a favoured habitat.

STONE CARVING DETAILS

  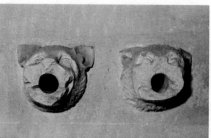

▲ In the first floor bathroom, two delicately carved panels, left and right above the fireplace, depict two contrasting views of natural history—left-hand panel, the innocent idyll of songbirds in the trees—right, possibly intended as more biblical in its emphasis, the serpent lurks among the fruits.

▲ The bath taps, carved animal heads, previously damaged, but since repaired. The bath is made entirely of stone

▽ A traditional vaulting boss, with a beautifully carved oak leaf cluster detail.

One of the vaulting bosses is a carved Green Man. Although believed to be a pagan motif, Green Man carvings are found in many churches, abbeys and cathedrals, which could explain Leigh's acceptance of the carving. ▷

▽ Carved vents that were architect Benjamin Bucknall's design 'trade mark'.

 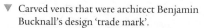  

▲ The Chapel's staff gallery, photographed in 1987, with its ornately carved front cornice that would have been visible only to the Leigh family in the gallery opposite. The staff's view across offered a much simpler, undecorated, detail.

◄ The Drawing Room's vaulted ceiling, photographed in 1992 after it had been cleaned and painted.

GARGOYLE CARVINGS

Gargoyle details, photographed from a 'cherry-picker' platform.

▲ One of five gargoyles on the south elevation, all restored and fully functional as rainwater spouts.

FAMILY FORTUNES

History repeats, as three families — over a period of two centuries — struggle to establish their respective visions of a country estate in Woodchester Park.

"A magnificent property — a princely desmene — 4000 acres of excellent land."

An 1840 sales advertisement for what was then known as the Spring Park Estate - soon to be Woodchester Park.

The Woodchester area has a long history of habitation that certainly dates back to Roman times — as evidenced by the world-famous Woodchester 'Orpheus' mosaic, which, at some 15 metres square, is the largest in Britain, laid in the early 4th century within a massive palace, unearthed in the late 18th century by Samuel Lysons. Under various titles, nearby Woodchester Park has been the home of landed gentry since Elizabethan times. During Elizabeth 1's reign the estate was granted to the Huntley family by the Crown and the family sought to establish a deer park. Failing finances forced them to sell the estate to Sir Robert Ducie in 1631. Several generations of his family gathered together a massive country park estate and built a period piece Georgian mansion, but they too were obliged to sell, this time to William Leigh in 1845.

With what seems to be a degree of inevitability, three generations of the Leigh family failed to realise their own ambitions in the secluded Woodchester valley. When the estate was finally sold in 1939 by his elderly spinster grand-daughters, William Leigh's Gothic mansion — the personal focus and expression of his religious devotion — stood empty and unfinished. The story of Woodchester Park as a country gentleman's estate ended much as it had begun — with a family's wealth consumed by over-ambitious projects in this uniquely secluded valley.

▲ The Tower – which remains as a habitable dwelling – is thought to have been built by the Ducie family in the 17th century.

▲ Its dominant position can be judged from this photograph, taken from its rooftop, looking down the valley along the string of artificially created lakes, towards South Woodchester.

The Orpheus Pavement: details of the original 4th century mosaic, laid in a massive Roman villa in Woodchester, photographed by Margaret Lister in 1973 when the pavement was last uncovered.

The restored Boat House: built on the third lake — Brick Kiln, Old and Middle ponds are the first three of a chain of lakes created by the Ducie family by the middle of the 18th century. ▶

Woodchester Park: a history of its development as a country estate

In 1564 the Huntley family from Frocester had set about creating a deer park. By 1610, through purchases and the enclosure of common land, a massive estate had been assembled. Its size can be gauged by the existence of a seven-mile long wall around the boundary and there was a hunting lodge at the western (Nympsfield) end. The expense of this venture reputedly put the family on the verge of bankruptcy.

In 1631, the Huntleys were forced to sell the park and the manor to Sir Robert Ducie. He, and subsequent generations of his family, worked to create a magnificent landscaped park out of the Huntley's deer park and build a grand country house. The Ducies decided to extend and adapt the hunting lodge and the house called Spring Park was built during the 1740s; by 1750 it was finished, when Frederick, Prince of Wales stayed there.

In 1788 George III visited the estate, and before the king's visit, work had begun on extensively re-landscaping the grounds, removing formal gardens to create a naturalistic park, based on plans by John Speyers, an associate of Capability Brown (1716-1783). Part of their scheme was to dam several small fishponds to form a series of lakes — works carried out in the late 18th, or early 19th Century.

The house was also remodelled several times in the 1770s and 1830s — including the reintroduction of a formal garden area by Humphry Repton. However, in 1840 when the 2nd Earl Ducie wanted to carry out further alterations and repairs, the estimate for the works proved to be too great. History repeated itself and the 4000-acre estate was put on the market.

Copies of the original advertisement describe the Ducie mansion as a *"magnificent property"* with a *"princely desmene"* and *"4000 acres of excellent land"*.

1845: the Leigh family arrives at Woodchester Park

In 1845, William Leigh bought the Woodchester estate for £170,000 (*the modern day equivalent is approximately £10.25 million*). Leigh's father — also named William — had been a wealthy merchant, born in 1754, who had made his money from trading tobacco and salt out of Liverpool. His son was born in 1802, rather late in his father's life and when he duly died, young William was just 13, inheriting £100,000 (*£6 million*) and the family estate near Liverpool. In his will, William's father had left instructions for his son's education: *"I wish my Son to have a liberal allowance for his Maintenance and Education and his Education to be such as to fit him for the Society of those with whom his ample fortune will afford him the means of associating."*

So young William went to Eton, matriculated in 1819 — then the equivalent of GCSEs — and attended Brasenose College, leaving without a degree in 1822. He grew to be widely travelled (often with his mother), fluent in Italian and acquired interests and property in Australia. In 1828, William had married Caroline Cotterell — the fifth daughter of Sir John Geers Cotterell — and they set up home at Little Aston Hall, Staffordshire. They had four children one of whom, a son, James Henry, died after eight months, while both his daughters predeceased him: Caroline Blanche died of TB in 1852 aged 21 and Beatrice Catherine in 1867 aged 32. Only his son William — referred to as Squire Leigh, or Willie — was left to carry on the line and further his father's vision.

So, why did William Leigh — seemingly well established at his family home in Staffordshire — buy the Woodchester estate, some five years after it had been put on the market?

The overwhelming impetus for the Leigh family's move from Staffordshire to Gloucestershire came from William Leigh's conversion to Catholicism on March 10th 1844. After his conversion, Leigh was reputedly 'given the cold shoulder', ostracised by his neighbours and former friends, and sought to move to an area devoid of Catholic influence, there to establish a new and significant Catholic community. His choice was Gloucestershire, more specifically the south Cotswold villages of Woodchester and Nympsfield — some 4.5 miles (7 kilometres) apart — an area where there was no Catholic presence within a radius of about 16 miles. Here he sought to create a new Catholic community and establish a centre from which the recently emancipated Catholic faith would spread.

While Leigh was still living in Staffordshire, he had established contact with two figures who would prove to be of major significance in the story of his move to Woodchester and the building of the Mansion. One was an influential architect, the other a charismatic Friar,

▼ The original Lodge — since demolished — at the Woodchester entrance; the stone gateposts, similar to those still in place at the Nympsfield entrance, have been removed.
Reproduced courtesy of the National Trust.

▼ The old Kennels, of which only the open barn in the foreground remains today, close to the lower lakes.
Reproduced courtesy of the National Trust.

both fervent Catholics, both single-minded and persuasive.

In 1842, Friar Dominic Barberi had moved to nearby Aston Hall, looking to establish a Passionist monastic community in England. Their arrival in Staffordshire provoked considerable antipathy, just as Leigh's conversion to Catholicism would do two years later—and this opposition came from Protestants and, surprisingly, local Catholics—who feared an upsurge of persecution against them. Friar Barberi has been cited as the direct inspiration for William Leigh's conversion, reputedly having instructed him in the Catholic faith. Other sources maintain that the two men only shared an acquaintance, or even that they never met while in Staffordshire. Wherever historic reality lies, Barberi would later opt to move from Aston with a view to joining Leigh in establishing his dreamed-of Catholic monastery in Gloucestershire.

The architect and designer was AWN Pugin—another zealous Catholic convert—who was working at Alton Castle in Staffordshire. Leigh commissioned an expensive silver chalice and monstrance for his local church from Pugin in thanks for his reception into the Catholic Church. This must have been an important contact, as Pugin—who

had converted to Catholicism ten years earlier—was an obsessive supporter of the Gothic style, which he believed to be the only true architectural expression of his faith. His impassioned and widely published opinions almost certainly convinced Leigh and determined the form and style of Woodchester Mansion.

In January 1846, Leigh asked Pugin to survey the existing Georgian-style Spring Park Mansion, presumably looking to improve the house for his wife and family. Pugin visited Woodchester and condemned the existing Georgian-style building, saying *"...a more hopeless case of repairs I never saw."* It is unclear whether this view reflected the true condition of the house, or, given Pugin's rejection of an architectural style he saw as 'Pagan', was a dismissive justification for its demolition. In a letter to the Leighs dated February 1846, Pugin set out his emphatic recommendation:

"...I have no hesitation in stating that it would be far more expensive to repair and alter the present building than to demolish it and erect a suitable residence...It is wretchedly built...Moreover the house is wretchedly designed...it is cold gloomy and cheerless..."

The architect promptly sent Leigh an estimate of £7118 (£427,000)—and a design for a new house. According to

architectural historian, Nicolaus Pevsner, Pugin subsequently asked to resign the commission for reasons of *"pressure of work"*, a plausible excuse, as work was then in progress on his most famous project, designs for the interiors of the Houses of Parliament. Another suggestion for his rejection of Leigh's commission is that Pugin, a widower since 1844, had been so distressed in the summer of 1846 by the refusal of his marriage proposal to Mary Amherst—she chose to become a nun—that he subsided into the period of ill-health that led to his premature death at the age of forty. However, Leigh's apparent reluctance to pay the amounts estimated by the architect is seen as another, possibly more substantial, explanation for Pugin's departure. When it came to his own works, the architect was fixedly opinionated and he was never short of commissions—he could doubtless afford to pick and choose...

A possible hint of Pugin's attitude to Leigh's hesitancy is to be found in the summary paragraph of his first estimate for demolition and rebuilding:

"I have no doubt you will think it a great deal of money but it is far better for me to give you a true and correct statement before you do anything... I am not

*aware that I have overlooked anything.
I am quite satisfied that you may turn
the key and light the fires, at the sum I
mention but no less..."*

Subsequent correspondence between Leigh and the architect becomes fractious, as Leigh followed up Pugin's first estimate with a tentative query looking to repair the Ducie's Georgian mansion, rather than opting to remove and replace it with Pugin's design. On 13th February, Pugin registers his disdain for such a suggestion in a letter to Leigh:

"If you thought it desirable to ascertain accurately the cost of entirely repairing the house, you might apply to a regular surveyor & then allow a good deal on the estimate for casualties."

Any falling out between the two was not yet terminal, for later that year, Pugin was called upon again by Leigh to initiate the building of the Catholic church, Our Lady of the Annunciation, and the associated monastery. It was a measure of Leigh's piety and devotion that, rather than begin by building his own family home in Woodchester, his priority was first to establish the two religious institutions he believed to be central to his personal vision of a new Catholic community.

▲ Hansom's monastery—occupied by the Dominicans, but originally built for the Passionists, who left Gloucestershire after the premature death of the order's leader, Dominic Barberi in 1849. The Monastery was demolished in 1970.

The diversity of the wider Woodchester community is highlighted in this pre-WWII photograph, with the industrial buildings of Newman Hender, shown in the foreground—one of several Woodchester mills and factories on a site that is now an industrial estate.

St Dominic's Church of Our Lady of the Annunciation, all that remains of the monastery complex ▶

The Church of
Our Lady of the Annunciation
and Woodchester Monastery

Despite their earlier disagreements over the design of the new Mansion, William Leigh turned to Pugin in 1846, asking the architect to design a new Catholic church, Our Lady of the Annunciation, and associated monastery at South Woodchester, adjacent to the eastern end of his estate. Pugin drew up plans for the church and monastery, but in August 1846 he again resigned the commission. One theory was that there was a disagreement over the church's siting, but this time Pevsner definitely attributes this resignation to a disagreement over the project's funding, and what Pugin saw as Leigh's intention to *"scale down"* the buildings. Pugin maintained that, as a result, the works would prove to be a *"miserable job"*.

Whatever the cause of this rift, Pugin left Woodchester and went back to his home in Ramsgate to build his own church — St Augustine's — where he would be buried just eight years later after a six-month illness (variously attributed to stress and overwork, or the effects of a cocktail of medication).

Leigh turned to another architect, Charles Hansom, a fellow Catholic, whose design for the church and monastery certainly follows William Leigh's exceptional passion for the Gothic style. Pugin visibly influenced Hansom's work, whose designs bore a distinct resemblance to Pugin's better-known buildings of that period; the church's interior detailing was compared at the time with Pugin's designs for the Houses of Parliament. Historian Pevsner describes Hansom's design as *"thoroughly Puginian..."* The foundation stone was laid in late 1846 and the church was consecrated and opened in October 1849 at a finished cost of £9,000 (£540,000).

However, just two months before the church's completion, on 27th August, the leader of Leigh's chosen monastic community, Dominic Barberi, suffered a heart attack at Pangbourne in Berkshire, while travelling from London to Woodchester. He was taken to the Railway Tavern at Reading, but died after being given absolution. With the untimely death of their leader, the Passionists decided to move on, to leave Gloucestershire, before the final consecration of Leigh's new Woodchester church and completion of the associated monastery. William Leigh offered the building to the Dominicans who were looking to establish a noviciate in England. They occupied the monastery until the 1960s, when dwindling numbers forced its abandonment and subsequent demolition in 1970, leaving just Hansom's church.

Even though it had no direct material connection with William Leigh, the final component of his dream of a new Catholic community — the Woodchester Convent — probably owes its existence to his spiritual vision and foresight. The convent was almost certainly established because Leigh's works elsewhere in the parish had helped to create an environment that was receptive to Catholicism. This convent was occupied by a closed order — the Sisters of Poor Clare — that arrived in Woodchester in 1860.

The Convent of the Poor Clares

"In all England there is not a more happy, devoted and loyal Community than the one at Woodchester..."

Bishop Lee — October 1945

The origins of the order date back to 13th century Italy — their founder, St Clare, was a wealthy Italian noblewoman, inspired by the preaching of St Francis of Assisi to live a life of faith, humility and poverty. The Sisters were a closed order, had no material possessions and led a

The Sisters of Poor Clares was a closed order, so when Margaret Lister was invited to record the daily life of the nuns, this presented a unique opportunity — here one of the sisters prepares the bread mix for the community's principal 'export' of altar breads.

The final production stage, where the altar breads are cut to shape.

◀ A picture of quiet contemplation – in the convent kitchen.

contemplative life in almost total silence *"to promote an atmosphere of prayer"*.

The order decided to establish a Poor Clares community in Woodchester and their chosen site included an existing 17th century house which the first 16 nuns occupied in 1860, finding the old building to be "in a very unfinished state". Work on the design of the new convent began in 1861 and the architect, Charles Hansom, offered an indirect link to William Leigh, having taken over the design of Woodchester Mansion after Pugin had resigned the commission in 1846. In 1865, the nuns moved into Hansom's new convent complex, which included an orphanage, later a Catholic school which survives to this day as St Dominic's, albeit in different buildings close to Leigh's church.

All told, the Poor Clares occupied the Woodchester site for just over 150 years and in 2010 the community celebrated its 150th anniversary. However, with numbers dwindling it was decided to close the convent and in 2011 the remaining five nuns moved to the Poor Clares community in Devon.

In 2013, the convent building was sold for conversion to a boutique hotel, run by a family business.

▲ The Woodchester convent has no direct connection with William Leigh's vision of a new Catholic community in Woodchester, but the one link with the Leigh family was the building's architect, Charles Hansom, who was also responsible for the first stages of Woodchester Mansion's design.

The design and 'incomplete' construction of Woodchester Mansion

Leigh now returned his focus to the task of accommodating his family at Woodchester and commissioned his third architect, another Catholic convert, 21 year-old Benjamin Bucknall. Leigh had first met Bucknall through their connections with the new Woodchester church — Bucknall converted to Catholicism and was confirmed in the Church of the Annunciation on 2nd May 1852. Leigh was so impressed by Bucknall's interest in mediaeval art and crafts of the Gothic period, that he arranged for the young architect to be articled to Charles Hansom. Bucknall duly joined Hansom just as the older architect was finishing work on what by now had become the Dominican Priory, and starting on his new plans for Leigh's Mansion.

The family had moved into Woodchester Park House (now known as Easter Park House) an extended gardener's cottage, that the Leighs renamed, 'The Cottage', located above the Mansion on the ridge to the south. Hugely altered and extended over the years, ultimately growing to become a 16-bedroom country house, 'The Cottage', would prove to be the family's main residence as work on the Mansion stuttered and faltered.

▲ This 1989 photograph, taken from a glider, connects the two Leigh family dwellings — with the mansion (lower) and (above) 'The Cottage', the euphemistically named 16-bedroomed country house that the family occupied throughout – and beyond - the period of Woodchester Mansion's construction.

Around the mid-1850s, Leigh's young protégé, Bucknall, was handed the job of completing the design for the Mansion, probably working under the auspices of Hansom's practice. There remains some debate as to the full scope of Bucknall's involvement — he may well have added interiors and details within Hansom's external fabric; certainly, Hansom had already designed the North Range, essentially the house's service area, with kitchen, laundry and servants' rooms.

What is apparent is that when it came to the design of his Mansion, Leigh was looking for something extra — one stated reason for Bucknall taking over from Hansom was because Leigh believed the younger architect to be capable of more 'flamboyant design'. There is a marked difference between the respective areas known to have been designed by the two architects; Hansom's north range contrasts with the High Gothic style of the east, west and south ranges, attributed to Bucknall. This contrast in style and decorative detail is visibly beyond the required functionality of the North range and the rest of the accommodation.

By 1858 the Mansion's clock tower had been completed, and by 1866 the main building had been roofed. In its heyday there were over 100 people of varying trades working on the site - many of their hand tools were found where they were left around the building in the late 1980s.

The family remortgaged the estate in 1870, to raise the sum of £10,000 (*£500,000-£600,000*). But, by the time William Leigh died—in 1873—building work on the unfinished Gothic-style Woodchester Mansion had ceased. The only work of any significance to be carried out after Leigh's death was the completion of the Drawing Room for a visit by Cardinal Vaughan in 1894.

After the death of his father, Squire Leigh moved back to Woodchester Park and continued to live in The Cottage above the valley for a number of years with his family of five children—eldest son Francis William, sisters Blanche and Beatrice, Henry Vincent and youngest son Bertrand.

After 1873: the end of the Leigh family's century of influence in Woodchester Park

Thereafter, the Leigh family of Woodchester quietly faded away—with no heirs, indeed no offspring at all, after the birth of Squire Leigh's youngest son, Bertrand Charles Leigh, in January 1871.

Bertrand joined the Army in 1890, becoming a 2nd Lieutenant, then left

▲ Recorded as being completed in 1858, the clock tower stands centrally within the west elevation and, top right, the old clock face; lower right, the renovated clock. The inscription reads 'IN SAPIENTA AMBULATE TEMPUS REDIMENTES' — 'Walk in the ways of wisdom, redeeming the time' (Ephesians 5, 15-16).

Perhaps one of the most explicit records of the parlous state of Woodchester Mansion in 1987 is this photograph of the roofs over the North Range. ▷

for Australia, where, at the age of 30, he married Frances Maude, a widow with one child. There were no children from this marriage and in 1910 Bertrand died from alcoholism in Melbourne.

When Squire Leigh died in October 1906, his eldest son, Francis, also an alcoholic, was deemed unfit to inherit the estate; his brother Vincent was, for the time being, overlooked, so their sister Blanche was made Woodchester's legal 'custodian' in their place. Her father believed her to be more capable, with a greater interest in the business of the estate, than younger brother Vincent. To compound the family's difficulties, just months after the death of his father, Leigh's son Francis William died unmarried in Barnwood Mental Hospital in January 1907. In the short term, double death duties for father and son, one almost immediately after the other, served to further deplete the family's dwindling resources.

Ironically, middle son, bachelor Henry Vincent, demonstrated some commitment to the estate. He went on to invest time and money in improving half a dozen farms, also adding a bathroom and garage to 'The Cottage', which he rented to tenants while living in London and Bath. He was also the only one of the family to actually live in the Mansion. He had some of the North Range servants' quarters at the rear of the house converted to a suite of rooms, in which he lived from 1907 for a number of years. Much to the annoyance of his two sisters, Vincent duly sold the estate in March 1922 for £52,000 (£2-3 million) and moved away to live in Chester, where he married, aged 56, in 1923 and died childless in 1928. His obituary described him to be "…of a retiring disposition and took no part in the public life of the city."

Neither of the Leigh daughters married. They lived for many years on the Woodchester estate in Scar Hill, a four-bedroomed lodge that still stands at the Nympsfield end of the track leading down to the Mansion. After the sale of the estate many of the outlying farms were sold off for profit; Vincent's sister, Miss Blanche, managed the rents from the five farms closest to the park. This arrangement enabled her to establish a possessory title to the central 1000 acres of the estate, including Woodchester Park and the Mansion. So in 1935 the Mansion again became the property of the Leigh family, but by this time Blanche Leigh was over seventy, and she sought to find a purchaser for the estate.

continued on page 38…

THE WORLD BEYOND WOODCHESTER PARK

Between the late 1840s and the early 1870s, the world outside the Woodchester Park estate was rapidly changing. As the Georgian period drew to a close, there was a massive acceleration in England's shift from a predominantly agrarian economy towards an overwhelmingly industrial economy.

In 1845, the year William Leigh bought the Woodchester Park estate, several events took place that serve to illustrate the way that the wider world was changing.

In May 1845 the railway reached Stroud, part of the Cheltenham and Great Western Union Railway: between 1830 and 1850, about 6000 miles of railway lines were built in Britain. In August, Isambard Kingdom Brunel's steamship Great Britain arrived in New York, the first screw-propelled vessel to cross the Atlantic, a ship built of iron, powered by steam and fuelled by coal. In September, Ireland's Great Famine began with an outbreak of potato blight, an agricultural disaster that led to mass emigration to England and the Americas, providing the 'navigators', or navvies, whose mass manpower was essential to the digging of the canals and the building of railways that transported the raw materials for, and the goods produced by, the country's newest and fast-growing industries.

Possibly the Leigh family found themselves out of step with a world that was shifting far beyond their familiar field of experience? To compound any effects of this economic shift, there was a short but severe trade slump from 1847 to 1848, coinciding with William Leigh's first attempts to design his country estate mansion. According to historian Eric Hobsbawm, this was: *"...the last and perhaps greatest, economic crisis of the ancient kind, belonging to a world that depended on the fortunes of harvests and seasons."*

This recession marked the end of an era. Throughout the hundred or so years of the Leighs' involvement with the Woodchester estate, the family seemed to cling on to the outmoded lifestyle of 18th century landed gentry. But, in the mid-19th century, old values and the 'old money' of an essentially agricultural economy, were overtaken and largely supplanted by the massive national and personal wealth generated by new manufacturing industries and associated commerce.

The long-established 'aristocracy' of gentlemen farmers and landed gentry found themselves pushed down the social scale by a different breed of self-made men — wealthy mill and mine owners, building contractors and tunnel builders, shipbuilders and railway speculators.

These were the new millionaires. They were building themselves grand mansions on the back of fortunes made in 'smokestack' industries. Their fortunes were often made by employing rural workers who migrated to the cities in their droves — the cotton industry took on 100,000 new workers in the 1850s. Some of the old landed gentry readily adapted to change — the Earls Fitzwilliam sank coal mines on their country estates in Yorkshire — but the Leighs never seemed to be part of the nation's irrevocably rewoven social fabric.

In 1873, the year of William Leigh's death, much of the industrial world had slipped into a major economic downturn which especially affected Western Europe, with Britain considered to have been hit the hardest. Unfortunately for the Leighs, living and working as they were in the 'old way' of a traditional country estate, their incomes were probably much reduced. The view is widely held that the economy of the United Kingdom remained in continuous depression from 1873 to as late as 1896, the early years of which coincided with Willie Leigh's attempts to move his father's mansion on to completion. But, within this economic context, this was not to be.

The Leigh sisters were well-known figures in the villages of Nympsfield and Woodchester, always known as the 'Miss Leighs'. They exerted a great influence on the religious life of the village of Nympsfield, in particular being instrumental in the founding and building of both the village's school and the Roman Catholic church of St Joseph's. Their involvement came at a price — they had to sell off most of what they still owned to pay for the two buildings. In 1938, they finally sold the Mansion, but not as Blanche Leigh had hoped to a religious order that would use the Mansion, and, especially, the chapel.

She had to settle for a sale to the mental institution where her brother Francis had died some thirty years before — Barnwood House. Ever the fervent Catholic, a reluctant Miss Leigh was persuaded to sell to them, bemoaning the fact that, *"the beautiful Chapel will now be used for non-Catholic worship"*.

The new owners considered Woodchester Park to be an excellent site and planned to erect new buildings for their patients and use the Mansion as offices. However, the hospital's plans for Woodchester were abandoned with the onset of war in 1939.

During the Second World War Canadian and American troops were

▲ The west Rose Window of Miss Blanche Leigh's "beautiful Chapel".

billeted in the park and were trained in bridge-building on the lakes in preparation for the invasion of Europe after D-day in June 1944. Understandably, security was high and rigorously enforced, and the Park was inaccessible to the general public. After the war, probably because the shooting rights were a source of income to the owners, visitors were discouraged — one old metal sign remains embedded in a tree on the west track, opposite the car park steps. Its barely legible message reads: 'Private - Keep Out'.

With the post-war deaths of the impoverished 'Miss Leighs' — Blanche in 1946 and Beatrice in 1949 — the line died out and the Leigh family's century of influence and involvement in Woodchester Park and the neighbouring village of Nympsfield finally came to an end. Thereafter, no significant events or developments affected or changed the Mansion's fabric, other than the deleterious effects of exposure to the elements. Despite having been classified as a Grade I Listed building in 1960, long years of neglect followed when the Mansion stood virtually forgotten, recklessly vandalised, sometimes used as a spooky 'adventure playground' by local children.

Then, in 1987 Stroud District Council bought the Mansion and thirty acres of land, the first step in rescuing the Mansion from dereliction. Later that year, Margaret Lister and her colleagues made their timely rediscovery of Woodchester Mansion. From these small beginnings came the Woodchester Mansion Conservation Group, the objective of which has always been to bring

▲ Woodchester Mansion stands cold and empty in the snow.

William Leigh's Woodchester Mansion to the attention of a wider audience and to maintain and conserve for posterity Benjamin Bucknall's masterpiece of Victorian Gothic architecture in its unfinished state.

WHY WAS WOODCHESTER MANSION LEFT 'INCOMPLETE'?

The Leigh's family history defines the themes that explain why Woodchester Mansion was conceived, designed and built—more particularly, the reasons why it was left unfinished.

From the outset, Woodchester Mansion's design and construction was beset with problems—the first architect, Pugin resigned the commission and progress on site was reputedly laboured—William Leigh was obsessively 'hands-on', finding it difficult to delegate, constantly involving himself with work on site, forever amending its form and detail. Throughout the process of construction, the Leigh family suffered flawed finances and some difficult family relationships; finally, with no children born after 1871, the family simply fizzled out.

Finance—or the increasing lack of it as work progressed—was probably the main reason why the building was never completed. The problems were apparent in the very early days of the Leigh family's involvement with Woodchester. The Leigh family's country estate lifestyle failed to generate sufficient income; indeed much of the family's wealth was consumed prior to starting on the Mansion, paying for the construction of Leigh's new church and monastery in Woodchester. In 1853, William Leigh took out a mortgage for £10,000, most likely to fund the building of the monastery and to start work on the Mansion. Family correspondence claims that Leigh himself had owned up to being 'in money difficulties'. In the late 1860s

▲ Typical of the careful repair work carried out by the Woodchester Mansion Trust, this gargoyle on the south elevation has been restored. Directly linked to the mansion, its ageing fabric and a future of material conservation are practical training courses for stonemasons, an essential component of the fundraising programme. The students produce crafted stone pieces tailored to make specific, necessary repairs to the building's fabric.

and early '70s the family was again struggling with finance—in 1870, William Leigh deemed it necessary to remortgage the estate.

Throughout this period, William Leigh's general health was poor. He was troubled with a chest condition and by the early 1870s his health was declining. When he died in 1873, his son Willie inherited the estate. The relationship between father and son had not been easy, for William believed his son to be irresponsible; Willie's limited inheritance came with strings attached.

Willie found himself with a life interest in the Woodchester estate, a barely adequate annual income given his large family, plus whatever profits that the estate might generate - but with absolutely no capital. On top of that there were the 1853 and 1870 mortgage repayments.

Leigh's death in 1873 coincided with the start of the first 'Great Depression', otherwise referred to as 'The Panic'—a worldwide recession, especially affecting Western Europe. Here in Britain the depression doubtless heralded a decline in the estate's earnings - for the landed and agricultural sectors of Britain's changing economy were the hardest hit.

After his father's death, Willie Leigh at least made some effort to find a way forward with the mansion and elicited the opinions of two architects—James Wilson of Bath in 1873, and then returned to Benjamin Bucknall in 1874. Wilson emphasised the dampness, the unhealthiness of a building jammed in against the north hillside:

"I consider the situation [of Woodchester Mansion] far from the best that might have been selected on the Estate; it is low, damp, and has much shut-in on the South, West and North; so that a free circulation of air is impeded. Its position is much too close to the high bank on the North, which will always keep the House damp..."

▲ The Kitchen interior, cleaned and restored by the Woodchester Mansion Trust.

He suggested either partial or complete demolition and rebuilding elsewhere in the park, and estimated that it would be £2000 (*£100,000*) cheaper to build a new house, rather than finish the mansion.

Bucknall held similar views and came up with the same preference—building a new house elsewhere. As for leaving the house unfinished, Bucknall believed that the half-built house would diminish the value of the estate:

"No ruin is more melancholy looking or produces sadder impressions, than that of an unfinished house—its existence would cast a perpetual gloom over the Park."

None of these suggestions was ever taken up by any member of the Leigh family. By the mid-1870s, they probably lacked the funds—and the will—to embark upon any further work, whether completing the mansion, or demolishing it and rebuilding elsewhere.

Given the reduced fortunes of the Leigh family, set against a national economy in deep depression from 1873 to 1896, it is hardly surprising that Willie Leigh's attempts to revive his father's project through discussions with three architects came to nothing. Sadly the Woodchester Mansion project died with its originator—certainly no significant work was carried out after 1873. And so Bucknall's unfinished building stands witness to Robert Browning's contemporary lament: *"the haunting curse of the artist — the incomplete"*.

THE FUTURE?

How can Woodchester Mansion be conserved? Can ongoing repairs and renovation maintain the building in its unfinished state, while improving on its parlous condition 'as found' in the late 1980s? What new directions could, or should, the Mansion Trust explore in working to secure the future of this unfinished Gothic-style masterpiece?

Under the management of the existing Trust—with a programme of vigorous and constant fund-raising and grant support—the aim is to maintain the mansion's material status quo at the very least. That in itself is a huge challenge. Woodchester's unique attraction as a half-built Victorian mansion is its material weakness. The unfinished fabric leaves the ageing building exposed and vulnerable to the elements. So what could the future bring?

The key to the future of Woodchester Mansion plainly lies in establishing sources of secure and enduring finance. But why should anyone bother? The answer is obvious. Here, hidden away among the valleys of the south Cotswolds, we have a unique Gothic-style masterpiece, an irreplaceable monument to a lost era and to a family's lost history.

In its unfinished state, the Mansion reveals all the innate honesty and integrity of Gothic masonry construction—the use of complex, but proven building techniques, based on the simple structural miracle of the pointed arch. Ornate carved bosses—including one depicting the mythical Green Man—gather together the ribs of complex vaults; still visible high up in unplastered walls, brick relief arches

The Drawing Room, the only room completed in the Victorian period in Woodchester Mansion. This is now the venue for functions, such as meetings, talks, charity dinners and weddings.

divert massive masonry loads around the visible, wide-span stone-arched openings below.

So the future of Woodchester Mansion has to be made enduringly certain and secure—it must not be allowed simply to rot away towards what would be inevitable dereliction for lack of will, energy or funding. New approaches and ideas, new backers and the recruitment of newly enthused supporters will all be essential to help secure this. Everybody

with an interest in Woodchester Mansion must play their part.

One of the ways of expanding the Mansion's funding 'portfolio' is by exploiting different ways in which the building can be used. Promoting its availability as a unique location is proving to be a positive policy—not just in terms of financial benefits.

An important by-product of this approach is that it widens the mansion's 'audience', bringing in people who might otherwise have no awareness of its existence, visitors who may well become enthused by the building and develop an affinity for this very special place.

Woodchester Mansion is available for hire as a venue for an ever-expanding range of commercial and social activities and events, offering various spaces with the atmosphere and character to suit every occasion.

The elegant, fan-vaulted Drawing Room on the ground floor *[previous page]* is the perfect setting for weddings, charity dinners and similar functions. More formally, the Drawing Room has been used for business seminars and specialist talks — including one given by local resident, author Evelyn Waugh, in 1938. There has been any number of TV paranormal programmes and organised ghost-hunting tours, when visiting groups tour the building in search of evidence of the supernatural — one televised event yielded a 'sighting' (or 'sounding') in the top floor Croft *[below left]* which turned out to be no more than an accidentally kicked pebble rattling against the wall. Down in the depths of the mansion's cellars, October revellers can find the perfect ghostly spot for their annual Halloween parties *[below centre]*.

The mansion's period character offers a distinctive, haunting setting for everything from photo shoots to fashion shows, one of which featured striking outfits by designer Vivien Westwood *[above right]*. This same atmosphere is ideal for dramatic theatrical productions

and other performance events *[left]*, whether indoors using different rooms and spaces, or outdoors, with the Mansion building standing proudly as a unique period backdrop.

Directly linked to the building's ageing fabric and to assist in its conservation, practical stonemasonry training courses are held at the Mansion. The students produce crafted stone pieces tailored to make specific and essential repairs to the building's fabric.